EXMOUTH

of Yesteryear

from the Docks to Orcombe Point

Kevin Palmer

OBELISK PUBLICATIONS

OTHER TITLES IN THIS SERIES

Ashburton of Yesteryear, *John Germon and Pete Webb*
The Teign Valley of Yesteryear, Parts I and II, *Chips Barber*
Brixham of Yesteryear, Parts I, II and III, *Chips Barber*
Pinhoe of Yesteryear, Parts I and II, *Chips Barber*
St Thomas of Yesteryear, Parts I and II, *Mavis Piller*
Ide of Yesteryear, *Mavis Piller*
Princetown of Yesteryear, Parts I and II, *Chips Barber*
Kingsteignton of Yesteryear, *Richard Harris*
Heavitree of Yesteryear, *Chips Barber*
Kenton and Starcross of Yesteryear, *Eric Vaughan*
Dawlish of Yesteryear, *Chips Barber*
Devon's Railways of Yesteryear, *Chips Barber*
Okehampton of Yesteryear, *Mike and Hilary Wreford*
Sampford Peverell of Yesteryear, *Bridget Bernhardt and Jenny Holley*
Sidmouth of Yesteryear, *Chips Barber*
Whipton of Yesteryear, *Chips Barber and Don Lashbrook*
Kingskerswell of Yesteryear, *Chips Barber and John Hand*
Torquay of Yesteryear, *Leslie Retallick*
Lympstone of Yesteryear, *Anne Scott*
Chagford of Yesteryear, *Chips Barber*
Dartmoor of Yesteryear, *Chips Barber*
Beesands and Hallsands of Yesteryear, *Cyril Courtney*
Beesands and Torcross of Yesteryear, *Cyril Courtney*

OTHER TITLES ABOUT THIS AREA

Exmouth in Colour, *Chips Barber*
Walks on and around Woodbury Common, *Chips Barber*
Ten Family Walks in East Devon, *Sally & Chips Barber*
Sidmouth Past and Present, *Chips Barber* • Sidmouth in Colour, *Chips Barber*
Along The Otter, *Chips Barber*
Topsham Past and Present, *Chips Barber* • Topsham in Colour, *Chips Barber*
Exmouth Century, Parts One and Two, *George Pridmore*
Exmouth and Budleigh Salterton People, *George Pridmore*
Entertaining Exmouth, *George Pridmore*
Exmouth to Starcross – An Ancient Ferry, *W. H. (Harry) Pascoe*
We have over 180 Devon titles; for a full list please send an SAE to
Obelisk Publications, 2 Church Hill, Pinhoe, Exeter EX4 9ER

Plate Acknowledgements

All pictures belong to Kevin Palmer apart from: page 4 (middle); page 7; the top four on page 8; page 29 (bottom); and the top two on page 30, which belong to Chips Barber.

First published in 2000, reprinted in 2002 by
Obelisk Publications, 2 Church Hill, Pinhoe, Exeter, Devon
Designed and Typeset by Sally Barber
Printed in Great Britain
by Colour C, Tiverton, Devon

© Kevin Palmer/Obelisk Publications 2000

EXMOUTH

of Yesteryear

from the Docks to Orcombe Point

This is a series of pictures, some postcard views, others photographs, that covers the coastal area from the Docks, at one end of the beach, to Orcombe Point, at the other. In between we learn a lot about why Exmouth is such a favoured place.

The resort's history spans a long period, even back to the times of the Romans. Apart from being an ancient fishing village, the port was also once an important shipbuilding town. Exmouth contributed ships for the fleet which took on, and defeated, the might of the Spanish Armada. The place assumed a very different appearance during the eighteenth century when it developed as a fashionable seaside resort and became the 'watering place' of royalty, the rich and famous. If you are 'new' to Exmouth then you may be in for a few surprises. If, however, you are a 'local' then you might find some memories revived in this nostalgic but short journey of just under two miles.

We'll begin at the Docks, which were not completed until 1865, the year after an Act of Parliament had been passed to authorise construction. The work was made easier because of the natural U-shape of the land or point. Prior to this it was known as 'Shellpit', perhaps the reason for the present name of 'Shelly Beach'. The long-established Exmouth to Starcross Ferry can be spied, just right of centre, as well as a number of tall-masted sailing craft.

With the Docks came a large number of small firms, some directly involved with imports and exports, others related to ships and shipbuilding. Vessels came from far and near and the pubs in the vicinity were often lively and 'colourful' places with foreign sailors, from a variety of ports and countries, seeking refreshment.

In the picture at the bottom (opposite) the well-known timber merchant of Wilson & Son can be seen. The area to the right of this scene has changed considerably since this photo was taken many decades ago.

In the picture below, which shows the entrance to the Docks, a steam train can be seen heading towards Exmouth on the far side of the Exe estuary.

The aerial view above shows the Docks when they were a commercial venture. The 'holiday homes' of the Shelly, seen from both angles, have also gone, as has the Pier Pavilion, a reflection of the changing times in this part of the resort.

The picture below was taken in the early 1950s and gives an 'overview' of the dockland environment. The area surrounding this inlet, the flattest part of a fairly hilly town, has undergone immense change. For many years the dwellings of the Shelly Beach, shown opposite, provided holiday homes for many regular visitors and their friends. Some of these chalets or boathouses were lived in all the year round.

But as these pictures show, the times they were a-changing and the entire face of the Docks area at Exmouth was to alter through the 1990s. Dereliction was eventually followed by demolition. In the first year of mass destruction hundreds of thousands of poppies colonised this area and it was a scene of immense colour for a while. The area has been extensively redeveloped and not without its share of controversy, locals fiercely fighting to preserve their rights of access to Shelly Beach. Where humble abodes once overlooked the Docks and Exe estuary, now tall blocks of luxury apartments enjoy that privilege.

Not a car in sight! A young lad sits astride the sea wall, an almost mile-long limestone structure which had its foundation stone laid on 30 August 1841. It required 70,000 cubic feet of stone, cost £20,000 and was paid for by the lord of the manor, Lord Rolle. Drifting sand still continued to be a perennial problem so a parapet was added in 1868. It originally ran as far as the Coastguard Station but was extended to the length seen today in 1913. Before it was built high tides would reach a point in Alston Terrace, at the back of the Grove public house.

Below is Mamhead View as seen on a postcard sent in October 1906. Before these buildings were constructed Thomas Dixon had an extensive shipbuilding yard which ran up to this part of the resort.

The sea wall can be seen stretching away into the distance with its graceful curve visible in both of these yesteryear views. Being located just ten miles to the south of Devon's county town, Exmouth was well-placed to receive the hordes of day visitors from Exeter, most of whom arrived by train. As modesty seemed to be the name of the game, changing tents were a feature of the beach scene. In the 1920s it was forbidden for men to swim topless and as late as the 1930s it was a contravention of a by-law to change on the beach without doing so in a bathing tent.

The walk along Exmouth's sea front or Parade is a pleasant pastime, one which has been enjoyed by many people for a great many years. The triangle from the Point to the Lifeboat House and back to the Docks is the driest part of Devon, so there is always a good chance of a pleasant perambulation.

In the picture above two youngsters sit astride donkeys ready for a short ride along the beach and back.

Those wanting an ice-cream (or 'hokey-pokey' as it was then known) could buy it from Capucci & Sons, whose ten-foot-long barrel is shown above at the roadside in the middle distance. This small firm was the first Italian vendor in the resort. In those halcyon days the largest 'lump' of ice-cream was a penny. Mr Deangelis, another street salesman, arrived in 1904 and in addition to ice-cream he had carts or barrels selling hot potatoes and chips. Until 1913 a lamplighter was paid to cycle around the streets with a pole and a burning taper lighting each lamp one by one. He became redundant when the first electricity supply station was opened at Marpool Hill, some 14 years after it had been first discussed, just before the First World War.

In the bottom picture a vendor is taking his wares, which include fishcakes and oysters, along the seafront, no doubt in the hope of a profitable day. Morton Crescent, in the centre distance, was built in 1870, a year after the Imperial Hotel. In 1892 there were plans to build a bandstand close to Morton Crescent, but local opposition was so fierce that the scheme was abandoned. Years later one was built in the Beach Gardens, which we will encounter later in this book.

Again not a car in sight in these two views; just an occasional horse and trap, and a bicycle in the bottom picture. Cycling must have been a much more pleasurable experience in those halcyon days.

On the left side of the picture below two workmen can be seen up a ladder giving attention to a lamppost. In the distance the tip of Dawlish Warren can be spied. In those days it extended to a point much closer to Exmouth Docks and hence was also referred to as Exmouth Warren. A large number of substantial summer dwellings existed on this end of the sandspit, their needs being catered for by various Exmouth ferrymen. Note the regularly placed trees along the road – it is presumed that as the trees are shorter in the view above, it is older than the one below.

The view above looks westward towards the distant escarpment of the Haldon Hills, which have a much higher rainfall than sheltered Exmouth. The former Pier Pavilion, close to the dock entrance, can be seen.

Below the view is from a much higher point. At the very bottom of the picture is the Lifeboat Station, whilst towards the top right the houses which line The Beacon are just visible on the edge of the photo. The trees along the right side mask the former sea cliffs, which the tides used to reach in the past.

The Imperial Hotel was built in 1869, a year before nearby Morton Crescent, and had an assembly hall added in 1883. It was the victim of a major fire in more recent times and had to be largely rebuilt. On the left side of the top and bottom pictures there is a glimpse of the replica of the Temple of Theseus at Athens. There were originally two, the other being the Temple of Winds which was demolished. These unusual structures were built about 1824 and predated the hotel by almost half a century. The land on which they stood was appropriately known as Temple Fields.

Above is The Beacon, which dates back to the late eighteenth century, when the first terrace of six large houses was built. Lady Nelson occupied No 6 from 1801 and is buried in Littleham churchyard. Lady Byron, wife of the famous poet, resided at No 19 in the days when it was a hotel. There were so many of the 'gentry' staying in Exmouth that it was regarded as an extremely fashionable resort: other 'residents' included Lord Bute, Lord Teignmouth and Lord Guildford. Balls were an essential part of the social scene and were staged for a variety of excuses – victories, coronations, royal births and birthdays – and any opportunity for a gathering was grabbed. A list of those present was usually published and at times Exmouth had more aristocrats than ordinary folk, or so it must have seemed! A report for 13 September 1814 bears this out: *This health inspiring spot is at present overflowing with fashionables and the polite residents unite with the gay visitants in contributing to the social hour. Private Balls, public assemblies, water parties and sea-side rambles ... form a perpetual source of amusement and attraction.* In 1883 the port lights were erected here to enable fishing boats and other vessels to enter the port at night.

Below is Madeira Walk, a pleasant sheltered walkway which follows the line of the base of the former sea cliffs.

Exmouth of Yesteryear

Exmouth of Yesteryear

EXMOUTH, THE BEACH

The picture which spans the middle pages shows The Point and the Exe estuary behind it. Holy Trinity Church makes a fine landmark on the right-hand side of this aerial picture.

The card above, when posted to Nellie Smith of Honiton, was rather unseasonal: *With best wishes for a happy New Year to all, I hope Granny is better.* Asssuming that the view on it was taken on a fine summer's day, it shows that most beach visitors dressed up rather than down.

The picture below, which is before 1897 (no clock tower!) shows Channel View, once a hotel, now a café, on the right of the scene. Also shown are small sand dunes where there are now none. This rare picture postcard reveals a more peaceful place than the one above and the two opposite.

In these two similar scenes the Beach Gardens are a new attraction to the delights of Exmouth's fine and increasingly popular sea front. The number of umbrellas and protective headwear in the bottom picture shows that Victorians and Edwardians very wisely liked to shade themselves from the direct rays of the noon-day sun. The sender of the above card obviously benefited from the visit to Exmouth, for he wrote: *I am feeling stronger and better for the change. For the first time since I came it is raining this afternoon ...* For the record, Exmouth's sea front is one of the driest places in the entire county of Devon!

The angles of the views are similar but the top one shows the Tennis Grounds, whilst the bottom picture looks to the right of this and takes in the Beach Gardens, laid out in 1911, and the beach. The top scene predates the building of the Pavilion, and the horse-drawn conveyance seems to be ignoring the need to progress on the left-hand side of the road. A number of spectators are peering over the tall wall to catch a glimpse of the action. It is believed that the first recorded tennis tournament took place here in 1881, whilst the last was staged in 1922. At its peak this event was regarded as the leading one in the entire country outside of Wimbledon. Below, the ornate bandstand almost takes centre stage. Opposite are three more views of the Beach Gardens, two of which show the bowling green which was once located here.

The Bowling Green.
Exmouth.

Exmouth of Yesteryear

These two pictures show the distinctive tower of the Harbour View Café, once the home of the Exmouth Yacht or Sailing Club. Prior to this it housed salt-water baths, and offered such delights as Turkish and thermal baths, massage and so on. Deep wells were sunk here to create a supply of salt water. This is how the 'Bath House Café' was advertised in a mid-twentieth century Exmouth guide book: *Approached from the town by the pleasantly-wooded Plantation, or Bath Road, the café occupies a premier corner site in the centre of Exmouth Sea Front, convenient to the Pavilion, Swimming Baths ... etc. Bath House has long been part of Exmouth's historical tradition. In the early 1800s it was the centre which drew many fashionable visitors who came to Exmouth to enjoy its then famous saline baths. Recently restored, yet preserving an old-world atmosphere and charm, Bath House has again become a place of attraction where the discerning visitor or resident may dine in pleasant surroundings and find excellent food served under the personal supervision of the Head Chef ...*

The bottom picture, opposite, shows the former boathouses which were close to the rear of the Lifeboat Station. Above that are two pictures of the former open-air sea-front swimming pool.

The RNLI station is open to the public to see their work and all donations are gratefully received and well used. Their presence in the resort has been a long one and many have been thankful for their services. The *Catherine Harriet Eaton* was the first motor boat and arrived on 1 August 1933, purchased from a legacy of the Rev Charles Pemberton Eaton of Milford Haven. Eight thousand people attended the boat's christening at the end of that August. The *Maria Noble*, which succeeded her, was christened on 1 September 1954 and saved some 35 lives before being relocated to Blackpool, where she served until 1970. These pictures show these two boats and feature various personnel.

The *Maria Noble*, in service from 1953 to 1960, was involved in numerous incidents. One dramatic episode happened on Christmas Day 1956 when the 336-ton *Minerva*, a Dutch motor vessel, set off distress flares four miles off Orcombe Point. A south-east gale had whipped seas into a frenzy and huge waves swept the lifeboat as she made her way to the rescue. Unbeknown to the rest of the crew, William Carder, whilst attempting to go aft for shelter was washed overboard. Another huge wave struck second coxswain Jack Phillips and sent him flying over Brian Rowsell's head into the mizzen mast and then into the sea. A quick headcount showed two were 'missing'. The lifeboat ploughed on with its mission, sending a message back to shore to tell of the accidents. A search party found Jack Phillips, who had made it to shore. After a spell in hospital he made a good recovery. However, William Carder, landlord of the Volunteer in Chapel Street, was found face down in the water. All efforts to revive him failed. To commemorate his bravery and sacrifice Whitbread commissioned a new sign to hang outside his pub.

The top two pictures present different views of the former Coastguard Station, now the site of various 'attractions' for children to enjoy, including a boating lake. The bottom picture looks towards The Maer, once the home of the local golf links. Opposite is a fine aerial shot looking back along the way we have come in our sequence of yesteryear pictures.

Exmouth of Yesteryear

The top two pictures show the beach road, known as The Queen's Drive, when it was a narrow, 14-foot-wide thoroughfare with no sea wall, a sandy wilderness. The bottom picture shows a much more 'modern' view of it. This is from an age – the proverbial 'Good Old Days' – when there were few cars and parking, as well as driving, was a joy. The first car parking charges on Exmouth's sea front were made in 1933.

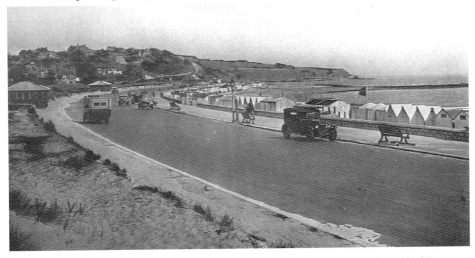

Exmouth of Yesteryear

The golf links are shown above, with the club house immediately above the head of the golfer about to play a shot. The golf links were on the Maer (Anglo-Saxon for 'boundary') and the slopes of Foxhole Hill. After the course closed the former club house served other functions including for many years that of Exmouth Zoo.

The Exmouth Golf Club has a sporting 18-hole course on the sea front, extending up the Littleham Valley. The Club fees are – Gentlemen: Entrance, two guineas; annual subscription, two guineas. A limited number are admitted for afternoon play at 10/6 per annum. Visitors: 1/- per day; 5/- per week; 10/- per month. Ladies: Annual subscription and entrance, one guinea, respectively. Visitors: 6d per day. The editorial didn't mention that the course was prone to flooding, as is still the case in the area around the picnic or barbecue tables. The course's demise came in 1957 when the Council, having seven of the holes under its control (the rest were rented from farmers) refused to renew its lease. A local by-law states the practice of hitting golf balls here is not permitted!

The large house behind the tree to the right of centre in the scene above was Shell House, the one-time home of the Victorian artist Francis Danby ARA. A native of Ireland, he came to Exmouth, from Naples, in 1841 and stayed until his death twenty years later. He brought with him an Austrian pine tree, which adapted well to his garden on the Maer. A sapling from this tree was planted during the Coronation celebrations of 1937 in Phear Park, near the old Marpool Hall. He is buried at St John-in-the-Wilderness, on the outskirts of Exmouth. As well as being a fine artist, he was also a keen boat builder, launching his vessels not far from Shell House. Sadly, the house was demolished in the 1920s. Had it remained, I think it would have made a fine museum or art gallery dedicated to his memory. But his name lives on in street names like Danby Terrace.

Exmouth of Yesteryear

If the prevailing winds are strong and blow for any length of time, vast amounts of sand accumulate on the sea front. The top picture shows the former subterranean toilets, which often had to be closed in winter and barricaded to prevent them being choked with sand. The Barn is shown below as it appeared in the early 1900s. Built in 1895, it cost £6,000 and stirred the imagination of many, as it had hidden passages and secret staircases. Much of the original building was destroyed in a major fire in 1905, the local brigade's appliance being regarded as inadequate to cope with such 'incidents'. It was rebuilt, its chimneys jutting prominently out against the skyline.

Throughout Exmouth's history there have been a number of shipwrecks recorded, and there are probably still several to be 'discovered'. This story is just one of the many; one which could hardly get overlooked, to judge by the number of 'witnesses' and the extent of the damage. The three-masted Russian schooner *Tehwija,* which had left the Finnish port of Hango, then in the empire of Russia, on 29 August 1907, had the great misfortune to shipwreck at Orcombe Point in October 1907. She encounted mountainous seas off Exmouth and started drifting towards land, half the cargo having already been washed ashore. The pilot was summoned but such were the dreadful sea conditions that he couldn't get close enough. Consequently she hoisted the distress signal. The local lifeboat, *Joseph Soames*, was called but it couldn't effect a rescue so the Teignmouth lifeboat, *Alfred Stamforth*, was launched. Its first rescue attempt almost ended in disaster when the crew were knocked over by a large wave and all their oars were washed overboard. It returned to harbour and the crew took a new set of oars and set about the rescue once more. This time they fared better and the *Tehwija*'s crew of eight were eventually taken off and transported to the Sailor's Rest. The ship wasn't quite so lucky and met her demise. Her cargo, strewn all along the shore, became salvage and was sold at auction. Here she can be seen in a sad and sorry state at the end of Exmouth's beach. The wreck provided a curious spectacle for locals, who were drawn to it in large numbers. Note the cliff at the back of the bottom picture: how different it looks today, after having been sloped off to reduce subsidence.

Exmouth of Yesteryear

We reach the end of our photographic journey of yesteryear along the Exmouth seaboard at Orcombe Point, where these two pictures almost reveal a 'before and after' situation. In the bottom picture the Marine Drive has arrived almost as if by magic. Orcombe Point's present café was built in 1966 and replaced a previous bungalow café that faced along the promenade. A storm not only did considerable damage to its structure but also brought down some of the cliff-face. The Army were eventually summoned and sloped the cliff back to a safer, less threatening angle. At the same time the zig-zag path or 'chine' that now ascends the cliff was constructed.

Exmouth, the resort, keeps its overall appearance but continues to change, in small ways, with every season. I hope that these pictures from the past will rekindle some fond memories and also form a visual record of how these two miles of golden sands, and their immediate surroundings, changed during the course of the twentieth century.

Exmouth of Yesteryear